THIS BOOK IS D
WHO SPEAK UP FOR THEMSELVES

For any inquiries please contact Crystal Hardstaff at
@thegentlecounsellor or hello@thegentlecounsellor.com

Notes for Parents, Caregivers, and People who work with Children

Teaching children about consent is an essential part of keeping them safe and healthy. It is important to start early and have age-appropriate conversations about what it means to give and receive consent.

Here are some tips on how to do so:

1. **Use appropriate language:** When discussing the topic of consent, it is important to use language that children can understand. Use simple terms.
2. **Teach children about personal boundaries:** Children need to understand that they have the right to set personal boundaries and that others should respect them.
3. **Emphasise the importance of communication:** Teach children to communicate their needs and feelings, and encourage them to listen to others when they speak.
4. **Talk about nonverbal cues:** Children need to learn to recognise and respect nonverbal cues, such as body language and facial expressions.
5. **Model respectful behaviour:** Children learn best by watching and copying their caregivers, so it is important to model respectful behaviour towards others.
6. **Encourage questions:** Let your child ask questions and encourage open and honest communication.
7. **Reinforce the message:** Reinforce the message that their body belongs to them, and they have the right to say no to unwanted touch.

Remember, teaching children about consent is an ongoing process, and it is important to have regular conversations to reinforce the message. By doing so, you can help to ensure that your child grows up with a healthy understanding of boundaries and consent.

My body is mine,
And I have a say,
About who touches me,
In every single way.

My body is mine, it's my choice,
I have the right to my own voice.

I love my little puppy,
And I show him I care,
But I always ask him first,
If a hug is okay to share.

I ask for consent, and listen close,
So everyone's boundaries are respected the most.

When I see all my friends,
We take turns when we play,
I ask if they want to join,
And if they don't, thats' ok.

They can say yes, they can say no,
It's up to them, that's how it goes.

Sometimes my tummy feels tight,
And my head feels all blurry,
So I tell my friends I need space,
And they respect my worry.

Respecting my choice is a must,
My body, my choice, it's how I trust.

I give a thumbs up,
Or a nod of my head,
If I want to keep playing,
Or it's time to go to bed.

Respecting my body and space,
Is important for a safe and happy place.

And when I'm with grown-ups,
I know they'll understand,
That if I don't want a hug or kiss,
They'll respect my demand.

I can give consent, and take it away,
It's my decision, every day.

So let's remember to ask,
Before we touch or play,
My body is mine,
And I have the final say.

My body, my choice, this I know,
And with respect, my confidence will grow.

OTHER BOOKS BY
CRYSTAL HARDSTAFF

The 'My Body' Series includes *'My Body is Mine'*, *'My Body, My Choice'*, and *'My Body is Safe'* by Crystal Hardstaff. These books are written for toddlers and young children to be introduced to and help them understand important topics such as the names of their private parts, body safety, consent, tricky people and safe people, and listening to their instincts. This book series was adapted and shortened from the author's original book *'Tricky People'* which covers all these topics and is suitable for young children to school-age.

For more information visit
www.thegentlecounsellor.com

18365633R00021